The Ble⸺ Enigma

200+ Facts on the Story of Alan Turing That Inspired the Smash Hit Movie *The Imitation Game* Starring Benedict Cumberbatch

Alan Johnson & Amanda Strickland

If you are a Benedict Cumberbatch fan, you are probably a *Sherlock* fan. As a "thank you" for purchasing this book I want to give you a gift. It is 100% absolutely free.

Please go to http://fandomkindlebooks.com/bletchley-park-sherlock-bonus/ to discover more fascinating facts about *Sherlock* and the smash hit BBC TV series created exclusively for you.

Disclaimer

Table of Contents

Introduction

Alan Turing was, until recently, one of the unsung heroes of the last century.

Unsung because much about him was shrouded in secrecy until the 1970s. It was then that the lid was finally lifted on the efforts of the code-breakers of WWII who spent their war years locked away at Bletchley Park working to break the infamous Enigma code and prevent the Germans from winning the war.

Winston Churchill called them his "golden geese" because in cracking the code, they gave us the golden egg and the ability to win the war.

With the veil of secrecy lifted, the world got to see just how much we had to thank the humble and quirky Turing for.

Born in the early part of the 20th century, Turing was a geeky and solitary child with a fascination for numbers and an intellect that was thankfully nurtured by his early caretakers and teachers.

The relentless logic that he applied to everything in his life perplexed those around him, but he stood his ground and showed unwavering confidence in his own abilities.

Churchill himself remarked that Turing's work at Bletchley Park during WWII was the single biggest contribution to the Allied victory.

Captain Jerry Roberts, who worked alongside Turing at this time, said that without him, we would have lost the war.

While we must never lose sight of the contribution of the thousands of men and women who worked at Bletchley Park during the war, we should perhaps be especially grateful that the single-minded perseverance of Turing prevailed at a time when the whole outcome of the war hung in the balance.

Join me as we delve deeper into the world of Alan Turing, an undoubted genius. Discover why the technology that we enjoy today is very much the result of the work and research that he dedicated his life to, how he contributed to the success of the Allies during WWII, and why his life story is the focus of Oscar-buzz following the release of the movie, *The Imitation Game*, starring actor-of-the-moment, Benedict Cumberbatch.

The Early Years

Alan Turing was born on June 23rd 1912 in Paddington, London, England.

He was the youngest son of Julius Mathison Turing and Sara Stoney. Alan's elder brother, John, went on to become a solicitor.

Julius worked for the Indian Civil Service (ISC), which led him to be away in India for much of Alan's childhood.

Julius wanted his sons educated in London, and so the boys spent their childhoods living with a retired Army couple.

As a young child, Alan attended Hazlehurst Preparatory School, where his tutors noticed his early aptitude and intelligence, and encouraged his desire to learn.

He became interested in chess while there and also joined the debate society.

In 1926, he moved onto Sherbourne School. There was a general strike in England that year, and so there was no public transportation. Alan had to cycle 60 miles to and from school. That was a pretty amazing feat for a young boy, but not too difficult for Alan, as he has an aptitude for fitness, later becoming an athlete of almost Olympic ability.

After Sherbourne School, he headed for Kings College at Cambridge University.

As a result of his dissertation proving the central limit theorem, he was awarded a fellowship of the college at the age of 22.

After leaving Cambridge, Alan furthered his education by studying mathematics and cryptology at the Institute of Advanced Study in Princeton, New Jersey, America. He was there from 1936 – 1938.

Turing was socially awkward, and it has long been thought that he may have had Asperger's syndrome (high functioning autism).

Authors and researchers into Turing have often compared his behavior to the Gillberg criteria, a set of six symptoms used to make a diagnosis of Asperger's. Most people have concluded that Turing did indeed fulfill all six.

These six symptoms are:

   Severe impairment in reciprocal social interaction.

   All-absorbing narrow interest.

   Impositions of routines and interests (on self and others).

   Nonverbal communication problems.

   Speech and language problems.

   Motor clumsiness.

In 1937, when he was 25, Turing invented the "Turing Machine," a theoretical computing machine that served as model for mathematical calculation. It formed one of the first, most important models in the study of theoretical computer science.

The War Years

The Government Code and Cypher School at Bletchley Park (GC&CS)

Bletchley Park had been purchased in 1938 by Admiral Sir Hugh Sinclair, who was head of the Secret Intelligence Service (SIS). The site had been bought with the outbreak of war in mind.

Bletchley Park's geographical location was one of the main reasons for its purchase. It was adjacent to Bletchley Railway Station and on both the Varsity Line (which linked both Cambridge and Oxford Universities), and the main West Coast line. Thus it was connected to all the countries main cities from London to Glasgow.

Good road links to London and the North East were nearby. The expected high volume of communications could be well-served at the telegraph and telephone repeater station in the nearby town of Fenny Stratford.

Commander Alistair Denniston was head of GC&CS from 1919 – 1942. Key cryptologists moved with him to Bletchley Park. They included those with backgrounds as linguists, chess players, and crossword experts.

After the outbreak of war, early recruitments came from both Oxford and Cambridge Universities.

Trustworthy women were drafted in to take up administration and clerical positions.

In 1941, a recruitment drive was undertaken with the newspaper, *The Daily Telegraph,* in the form of a crossword competition. Promising participants were then contacted with the offer of a "particular type of work to aid the war effort."

It was also recognized that formally trained mathematicians would be needed. Turing arrived at Bletchley Park the day after war was declared. He was joined by half a dozen or more of his peers.

Turing was housed in Cottage Number 3 and did all his early work from there. This was one of the intelligence "huts." It was here that translations and analysis of Army and Air force decrypts were carried out.

It was an eclectic mix of staff that worked together at Bletchley Park. They were affectionately labeled as the "Gold, Cheese and Chess Society."

Churchill had previously told Denniston to leave no stone unturned in his search for staff. Later, he told him that he hadn't expected him to take his words so literally.

By 1945, some 12,000 people had been assigned to Bletchley Park throughout the war.

Secrecy and security was paramount and discretion continually emphasized, even within Bletchley Park itself. It was frowned upon to talk about anything relating to Bletchley Park, and staff were advised to be cautious even within the huts themselves.

At the end of the war, Winston Churchill ordered that the Colossus computers (developed during the war), and the Bombe machines be destroyed to keep them from falling into the hands of the Soviet Union. Much of the paperwork was also destroyed. The secrecy surrounding the work was also kept in force. Many relatives whose loved ones had worked there never knew the true extent of what they had done. It was only in the mid-1970s that the veil was finally lifted, and people learned about Bletchley Park, the work done there, and the people who had done it.

Churchill said after the war that the staff at Bletchley were "the geese who laid the golden egg and never cackled."

Turing's Work at Bletchley Park

Turing turned down the opportunity to stay in America after studying at Princeton, and returned to Cambridge in 1938. He was immediately recruited into a part-time position at the Government Code and Cypher School to study cryptology.

During the war years of 1939 – 1945, Turing was involved almost completely with mastering the German enciphering machine "Enigma," with particular responsibility for deciphering U-boat communications.

His unique, logical decryption of Enigma resulted in him becoming the lead figure working on this project.

Further, in 1939, Turing developed an initial design for an electromagnetic device called "The Bombe."

The Bombe was used to discover daily settings from the Enigma machines used on various German networks.

The British effort to decrypt the Enigma was codenamed "Ultra." Their system eventually became the standard for all such intelligence amongst the Western Allies. Alternately, the Americans used the codename "Magic" for their decrypts from Japanese sources.

Turing became a top figure in Anglo-American relations. The Enigma project exposed him to some to the most advanced technology that was available at that time.

Much debate has been made as to the exact part that Ultra played in winning the war. Winston Churchill was quoted as telling the then King George VI that "it was thanks to Ultra that we won the war."

Official historians of WWII have written that Ultra intelligence shortened the war by up to two – four years, and that without it, the outcome of the war could have been very different.

Whilst at Bletchley Park, Turing struck up a good friendship with fellow co-worker Joan Clarke. He would arrange their shifts so that they could work together and later proposed to her. However, after admitting his homosexuality to her, he felt he could no longer go through with the marriage, even though Joan was said not to be shocked by the idea.

Turing later received an OBE in recognition of his work at Bletchley Park.

The Enigma Machines

The Enigma machine was created by German engineer Arthur Scherbius at the end of WWI.

Scherbius, however, was killed in a horse and carriage accident in 1929, long before his invention became famous.

Early models were adopted by the military in several countries, including Nazi Germany.

From 1938 onwards, additional layers of complexity were added to the machines, making decryption more and more difficult.

The basic operating system of the Enigma machines was simple. To send a message, the operator would set the machine to a combination known only to him and the receiving operator. He would then type in his message via the Enigma keyboard. This would then translate into different letters that would appear on a second upper board. This message was then sent via Morse code to the receiving operator. This operator would then set his Enigma machine to the same combination and type in the Morse code message. On his upper board he would then see the translation of the original message.

Most of the German cypher traffic was sent on the Enigma machines. Although they did have cryptographic weaknesses, when they were used properly, they were virtually unbreakable.

Attempts to break German Enigma codes began long before the outbreak of WWII.

In 1931, six years prior to the outbreak of WWII, thanks to Hans Schmidt, a clerk in the German code department, an Enigma operating manual and list of settings was smuggled out to French intelligence.

The French quickly realized that neither they, nor their British counterparts, could break the code, even with the manual and lists. So, they shared the information with Polish code breakers who were having better success at that time.

The Polish realized that the only way to break the code would be to create an Enigma machine, so they set about making one. They called it the "bomba".

In 1932, they achieved their goal and spent the following six years deciphering German messages, an achievement they didn't share with the French or British.

However, as the Germans prepared for war, they made several advancements to their Enigma machines which made continued deciphering impossible.

Just before Hitler invaded Poland, the Polish shared what they had learned in the six years previous. It was too late to save Poland, but the information they provided played an important role in Turing's development of "The Bombe," a machine that sped up the breaking of Enigma codes by eliminating the many incorrect possibilities.

By mid-1940, Turing and his fellow code-breakers at Bletchley Park were able to decipher messages within 24 hours. However, the most important messages, those sent by the German Navy, were still unbreakable to them.

It wasn't until a year later, in 1941, after a series of successful captures of actual German Enigma machines and lists, that a breakthrough was made, and German Navy messages were at last deciphered in real time.

National Physical Laboratory

After the war, Turing went to work at the National Physical Laboratory in Teddington, London.

He joined in October 1945. His time here was spent working on the pilot model of the ACE (Automatic Computing Engine).

In February 1946, Turing presented a paper in which he detailed the design for his first stored-program computer.

Although his design of ACE was very much feasible, due to the secrecy surrounding the post-war Bletchley Park, the project took time to gain momentum.

While at NPI, he produced a work entitled "Intelligent Machinery." His then employer at the NPI didn't like it and dismissed it as a "schoolboy essay."

It was finally published in 1968, 14 years after Turing's death, and was heralded as a far-sighted paper, looking at many of the concepts that were later to become central to the whole idea of artificial intelligence.

Turing became disillusioned with the slow speed with which his ideas were gaining acceptance. In 1947, he returned to Cambridge University for a sabbatical year.

While he was at Cambridge, a smaller version of his ACE design was built. It executed its first program in 1950.

Of the first production versions, 31 of the pilot ACE were delivered in the spring of 1955. It was known as the English Electric Deuce.

The full version that Turing had designed was never built, but a number of computers around the world owe much to his designs.

University of Manchester

In 1948, following his sabbatical year at Cambridge, Turing went to work at Manchester University as a "reader" in the mathematics department.

A "reader" denotes the appointment of a senior academic with an international reputation for research.

His work here was in the Royal Society Computing Machine Laboratory set up by Max Newman, a fellow code-breaker at Bletchley Park.

His work continued on software for early versions of stored-program computers.

The project he worked on here was called the "Manchester Mark 1."

He also continued his work in abstract mathematics, addressing problems with artificial intelligence.

The current School of Mathematics at Manchester University is housed in a building named after Turing. It was completed and opened in 2007.

In 2014 it was proposed in the UK Budget to build an Alan Turing Institute, to ensure Britain has a lead on the use of big data and algorithmic research. Manchester University is widely tipped to host this new institute.

Turing worked at Manchester University until his death in 1954. In 1950, he wrote a program entitled "Computer Machinery and Intelligence," where he introduced the "Turing Test."

The Turing Test

The Turing test proposed to test a machine's ability to answer as a human, or to be indistinguishable from a human.

The test does not seek to check the machine's ability to get the correct answer, but rather to test how closely a machine can mimic a typical human answer.

The test was inspired by the "imitation game." In this game, a man and woman are sent into separate rooms. They must answer a set of predetermined questions as if they are both women. The answers, which are typeset, are then read back to the other people present. They must decide which set of answers were provided by the woman.

Then Turing substituted a computer for one of the women. It was Turing's desire to see if inserting a computer into one of the roles would affect people's ability to judge whether the answers had come from a human or from the computer.

In the years following 1950, the test was both highly influential and much criticized. However it has since become an essential concept in the philosophy of artificial intelligence.

Manchester Mark I

The Manchester Mark I was one of the world's earliest forms of stored-program computers.

Work began on it in 1948, and the first version became fully operational in April of 1949.

Earlier versions of computers, such as the British Colossus (pioneered at Bletchley Park during the war), did not have the ability to store programs. For each fresh task to be carried out, it was necessary to re-route and re-configure cables and wires by hand and a series of switches.

It was Turing who conceived the idea that a program of coded instructions could be stored in the computer's memory and used instead.

The Manchester Mark I was primarily designed to allow researchers to gain experience in using computers in a practical way. However, the electrical engineering company, Ferranti, had been working alongside several universities with a view to producing a commercial computer.

Ferranti saw the possibilities with the Mark I and joined forces with Manchester University to produce a commercial version. The Ferranti Mark I was first released in 1951.

By this stage, Turing had withdrawn from involvement in the project. He had always been more interested in the possibility of producing computers that mimicked the actions of the human mind than he had in exploring their commercial possibilities.

Artificial Life

In his final years, from 1952 up until his death in 1954, Turing concentrated his work on artificial life and morphogenesis.

In general terms, morphogenesis is the biological process that causes an organism to develop its shape. It is often known as mathematical biology.

Turing's interest lay in the ability to use computers to study this process, rather than the laboratory setting of incubators, petri-dishes, and microscopes.

He continued to work out of Manchester University. As soon as the Ferranti Mark I was up and running, he began to use it for his investigations.

He published a paper in 1952, entitled "The Chemical Basis of Morphogenesis." The theory he detailed was finally experimentally proved 60 years later.

Further papers from this period in his life were published in 1992, and his contributions to the field were widely considered to be of vital importance.

Marathon Running

Turing had a lifelong interest in running that began when he was a young boy. Never a team player, he found in running something that was both solitary and competitive at the same time. He thrived at it. He became a keen marathon and ultra-distance runner.

From 1945 – 1947, while working for NPL, he was invited to run for Walton Athletic Club and quickly became their best runner.

Turing liked to run hard and fast, grunting loudly as he ran. When asked by a fellow club member why he ran so fast, he answered, "I have a stressful job, and the only way I can get out of my head is to run fast."

His best marathon time was 2 hours, 46 minutes and 3 seconds. At the time, it was only 11 minutes slower than the 1948 Olympic Games marathon winner.

Turing's Homosexuality

In December 1951, Turing met Arnold Murray.

Murray was a 19-year-old, working class boy. They met outside the Regal Cinema on Manchester's Oxford Street.

There followed a lunch date and an invitation to visit Turing's house, which Murray declined at the time.

They met again in January the following year and this time they embarked on an affair.

Murray later stole a "tenner" from Turing's wallet, and half convinced Turing that he hadn't. However, when Turing was later burgled, the suspicion fell on Murray.

When the burglary was reported to the police, fingerprints from the house identified a known thief, Murray.

Turing admitted that Murray was a friend of his. In his statement to the police, the true nature of Murray and Turing's relationship became clear.

Homosexuality was still illegal in 1952, and when questioned, a nervous Turing blurted out the truth.

He was arrested and charged with gross indecency.

The case came to trial in March 1951, and despite evidence defending Turing as a national asset for his work with computers and his OBE, he was found guilty.

Turing's work breaking the Enigma code in WWII was still considered "top secret" and was unable to be used as any part of his character reference.

Turing was offered two choices:
*   1. To serve a prison sentence.*
*   2. To undergo chemical castration.*

He chose the latter.

Chemical Castration

In 1952, homosexuality was still widely considered to be a "mental illness" that could be "treated" by chemical castration.

The idea was that it would reduce libido and therefore any sexual activity.

The drug cyproterone acetate (a synthetic female hormone) was commonly used. In Turing's case, it was given for a period of one year. After this time, the effects were largely thought to diminish, leaving the body to return to normal.

Some people suffered side-effects as a result of using this drug, and indeed Turing was one of those. The drug caused him to become bloated, infertile, and grow breasts.

He also started to suffer from bouts of depression. He started seeing a therapist during this time.

It would be another 15 years, 1967, before homosexuality between two consenting males over the age of 21 would become legal.

The Aftermath of Turing's Conviction and His Death

Aside from the sentence of chemical castration and the side effects he suffered as a result, perhaps the more serious effects for Turing were those relating to his work.

With a criminal conviction against his name, he found his security clearance revoked. This meant that he was barred from continuing any work connected with code-breaking and the Government Code and Cypher School, which by now had become known as Government Communications Headquarters (GCHQ).

Although no one can know for sure how this affected a mathematical genius such as Turing, one can only imagine that he was devastated to be unable to continue research into something he had dedicated his life to.

The following year, on June 7th 1954, Turing was found dead in his bed by his cleaner.

A half-eaten apple sat on the bedside table.

An inquest determined that Turing had died from cyanide poisoning, and although the apple was never tested, it was assumed that Turing had laced it with cyanide in order to commit suicide.

His mother and his friends disputed this. They claimed that he had accidently inhaled cyanide that he kept in a small room in the house and used in his experiments.

While we will never know the true facts surrounding his death, what is known is that the world lost one of its geniuses that day.

Royal Pardon

In 2009, John Graham-Cummings, a British programmer, began an online petition to get Turing a pardon. Over 37,000 signatures were eventually received over the course of five years.

Later that same year, the then British Prime Minister, Gordon Brown, issued a formal apology, citing the appalling treatment of Turing at the hands of the British government. However, he stopped short of asking for a pardon.

The petition and campaign gathered momentum, but in 2012, the hundredth year of Turing's birth, the then Justice Minister, Lord McNally, rejected the idea to formally pardon Turing.

This did nothing to dampen the campaign, and more and more people and many notable figures got behind it.

Professor Stephen Hawkins urged the Prime Minister to formally "forgive the iconic British hero to whom we owe so much as a nation."

The current Prime Minister David Cameron still rejected the idea of a parliamentary pardon, and thus the hundredth year anniversary of Turing's birth came and went without any justice for Turing.

It took until the end of 2013 for the Queen to step in and issue a posthumous pardon under the Royal Prerogative of Mercy. Although David Cameron had rejected the idea of a pardon only the previous year, he was now quoted as saying, "His action saved countless lives. He also left a remarkable national legacy through his substantial scientific achievements, often being referred to as the father of modern computing."

There have been only 43 Royal pardons since 1707.

The Alan Turing Centurion Year - 2012

The "Turing Year" marked 100 years since Turing's birth and involved many events in commemoration of the man.

Many of these events were linked to places that played an important role in his life, such as: Cambridge, Manchester, and Princeton Universities, and Bletchley Park. Events were also held all over the world to honor Turing's legacy.

A special committee, including Turing's biographer, Andrew Hodges, and his nephew Sir John Dermot Turing, was set up to oversee the celebrations.

Among the events organized was a four day academic conference held in Manchester University. It brought together many prominent and distinguished scientists of the day to discuss and analyze the development of computer science and artificial intelligence.

The Royal Mail included Turing in its 10 Britons of Distinction commemorative stamp collection, released in February of 2012.

Films, Books and Honors

Turing has long provided fascinating subject matter for many films and books about his life.

For one of the more important books on his life, we can look to author Andrew Hodges, who wrote the book, "Alan Turing: The Enigma." Michael Holroyd (an English biographer of distinction) chose this book to go on a list of books published in the British newspaper, The Guardian in June 2002 as one of their Guardian Essential Library recommendations.

Of the many popular films made to date about Turing's life, there is an award-winning drama documentary originally made for British TV. *"CODEBREAKER"* was released in October 2012 to coincide with the centurion year and has since been shown around the world garnering rave reviews.

Of the many awards given annually in reference to Alan Turing, the most significant has to be the ACM

A.M. Turing Award. It is an annual prize handed out by the Association for Computer Machinery (ACM) to an individual who contributes major and lasting technical importance to the computing world.

It is recognized as being the highest award available in computer science, the "Nobel Prize of Computing," and carries with it prize money of $250,000 and financial support from both Google and Intel.

The Imitation Game

Written by Graham Moore and directed by Morton Tyldum, *The Imitation Game* **is the new widely acclaimed and hotly anticipated film based on Turing's life.**

Much of the film centers on Turing's years at Bletchley Park and the race against time to crack the Enigma code.

Writer Graham Moore says that he has wanted to tell the story of Turing since Turing became his childhood hero at 14 years of age.

Moore adapted the screenplay from Andrew Hodge's book, "Alan Turing: The Enigma."

Moore also acted as executive producer on the film, which was four years in the making, meaning he got to see his project all the way through to the end.

For Norwegian director Morton Tyldum, "The Imitation Game" was his first foray into English speaking films. It is a task he seems to have executed perfectly as early reviews have been very good. There is already Oscar buzz around the film.

Benedict Cumberbatch plays Turing, and Keira Knightley plays Joan Clarke, the woman with whom Turing strikes up an unconventional love story whilst at Bletchley Park.

The film portrays Turing as a prickly, socially awkward character only too aware and completely sure of his intelligence.

Benedict shows a touchingly flawless portrayal of a man who had both a tortured and a beautiful mind.

Following the rounds at the film festivals (with rave reviews so far), "The Imitation Game" went on general release in November 2014.

To celebrate the opening of *The Imitation Game*, Bletchley Park is opening a new exhibition on the 14th November 2014.

Called "The Imitation Game," the exhibition will take visitors behind the scenes and into some of the very rooms where the film was shot.

The visitors will get to view costumes worn by the stars in the film as well as stand in the bar where not only filming took place, but also where Turing himself would come at the end of a long day.

Filming took place at Bletchley Park, which has been extensively preserved so that it is as it was during the war years.

All the stars of the film agreed that filming in the actual location where their characters had lived and breathed added a "ghostly" dimension to the whole experience.

Filming also took place at Turing's old school in Sherbourne, Dorset, in southern England.

Benedict Cumberbatch

Benedict was born on July 19th 1976 to parents Timothy and Wanda, in London, England.

His parents are also actors and have appeared with him on the TV, playing his parents on the popular TV series "Sherlock."

After leaving school, Benedict took off for a year to teach English in a Tibetan monastery.

On returning to England, he enrolled at Manchester University to study drama.

He has had a highly successful career to date, working in TV, theatre, film, and radio.

In 2004, he played the role of theoretical physicist, Stephen Hawkins, a performance that earned him a BAFTA nomination (the British equivalent of an Oscar).

Best known for his role in the TV series "Sherlock," Cumberbatch takes the lead role in

The Imitation Game, **a film that is fast becoming an Oscar hopeful.**

Many insiders are saying that the best thing about this film is Cumberbatch's performance, widely regarded as the best in his career to date.

According to those who have seen and reported on it, Cumberbatch brings together all of Turing's quirkiness and oddball habits seamlessly, creating yet another antisocial hero renowned for his genius.

Cumberbatch said of playing the role, "There was a huge burden and onus of responsibility. Turing was an extraordinary man who sadly and bizarrely was not that well-known for his achievements."

Cumberbatch reports that the actual moment in the film where the code is cracked for the first time gave him goose bumps. "I mean, literally, the hairs on the back of my neck stood up."

His research for the role was thorough and saw him scrutinize Enigma while it was on display at the Imperial War Museum in London.

Of Turing's pardon, Benedict says: "The only person who should be pardoning anyone is him. Hopefully, the film will bring to the fore what an extraordinary human being he was, and how appalling his treatment by the government was. It's a really shameful and disgraceful part of our history."

Of his performance in "The Imitation Game" he says, "Often you draw on your own experiences and memories, but I really didn't have to here. Turing got under my skin. It was just so pitiful. Imagining the physical weakness, the vulnerability, the exhaustion, how the hormones affected his emotional state. It was all ungovernable."

Cumberbatch has been known to bash the wildly successful drama, *Downton Abbey*, calling it "atrocious". He later claimed he was joking. His co-star in *The Imitation Game* is Allen Leach, who

plays Tom, the erstwhile chauffeur turned estate manager in *Downton Abbey*.

Pre-Release, Awards, and Oscar Buzz

Ahead of its general release in mid-November, *The Imitation Game* has done the rounds of the film festivals, where it has already started to pick up awards.

It made its world premiere at the Telluride Film Festival, where it easily proved to be the favorite film among the movie goers.

It won the People's Choice award at the Toronto Film Festival in Canada.

Over on the East Coast premiere in the Hamptons, it picked up the festival's Alfred P Sloan feature film award.

Other film festival awards *The Imitation Game* has received are:

Special Audience Recognition Award at the Aspen Film Festival

Best Gala Film at the San Diego Film Festival

Audience Award for Best Film at Scottsdale International Film Festival

Overall Audience Favorite at Mill Valley Film Festival

The Independent gave the film a 5-star review, calling it the best British film of the year.

In New York, the New York Post hailed it as a "thoroughly engrossing Oscar-caliber movie."

Other reviews describe it as:

"Beautifully written, elegantly mounted, and poignantly performed."

"Undeniably strong in its sense of a bright light burned out too soon."

"Strong, stirring, triumphant, and tragic."

Cumberbatch's performance has been described as 'a performance for the ages, proving he's one of the best actors working today."

Despite early reservations surrounding the film and how Turing was to be portrayed, his niece said that the film "really did honor my Uncle."

The Oscar buzz surrounding the film and Cumberbatch's performance is rife. It is widely acknowledged that this is one of his best performances to date, and that he brings Turing's own painfully, socially inept awkwardness to live in a way that has the viewer glued to the story.

Conclusion

There have been many geniuses throughout history. They seem to come at a time when the world needs them the most.

Alan Turing came at a time when Europe was going through one of its toughest struggles. That we came through it intact is undoubtedly because of the bravery of those who fought for their countries, and for the many who lost their lives doing so.

There were other heroes though, men who didn't put their lives on the line, but men who did everything in their power to help support those fighting on the front line.

Alan Turing was one of these men. A man of extreme intelligence who had to shout over those who doubted him, and push through with what he knew in his mind was the right thing.

In the film *The Imitation Game,* we discover just how loud he had to shout to prove that he could do what everyone was expecting him to, but in a way that very few understood.

After the war, Turing continued his groundbreaking work to develop the world's first computers. It is because of his early work that we sit here today in 2014 with an array of computer technology at our fingertips.

Throughout all this, he lived in a world and at a time when he was vilified for his sexual orientation. It seems madness today that a man could be arrested and found guilty of laws that made it illegal to love another man.

We can only imagine what a lonely life it must have been for him, unable to live and express himself freely. When the very work that he lost himself in was taken away from him, how must that have felt.

We may never know the true facts behind his death. Did he take is life or was it a careless accident? All we can know for certain is that the world lost out when Turing's life was cut tragically short. We can only sit and wonder what else he could have achieved had he reached his full potential.

His legacy lives on every day for every one of us. He was the father of computers. Every time we turn on our screens, we have to be thankful for the genius minds of men and women like Turing who push the boundaries, refuse to accept what is, continue to strive to learn, and push their brains to the limits and beyond. This, even when it is so very hard to get those not so intelligent and forward thinking to listen.

Don't Forget To Claim Your Free Gift!

If you are a Benedict Cumberbatch fan, you are probably a *Sherlock* fan. As a "thank you" for purchasing this book I want to give you a gift. It is 100% absolutely free.

Please go to http://fandomkindlebooks.com/bletchley-park-sherlock-bonus/ to discover more fascinating facts about *Sherlock* and the smash hit BBC TV series created exclusively for you.

Other TV and Movie Books

Available on Kindle and in paperback on Amazon:

Call The Midwife!: Your Backstage Pass to the Era and the Making of the PBS TV Series

Doctor Who: 200 Facts on the Characters and Making of the BBC TV Series

Downton Abbey: Your Backstage Pass to the Era and Making of the TV Series

Sherlock Lives! 100+ Facts on Sherlock and the Smash Hit BBC TV Series

Other Books:

KATE: Loyal Wife, Royal Mother, Queen-In-Waiting

HARRY: Popstar Prince

One Direction: Your Backstage Pass To The Boys, The Band, And The 1D Phenomenon